to Lin

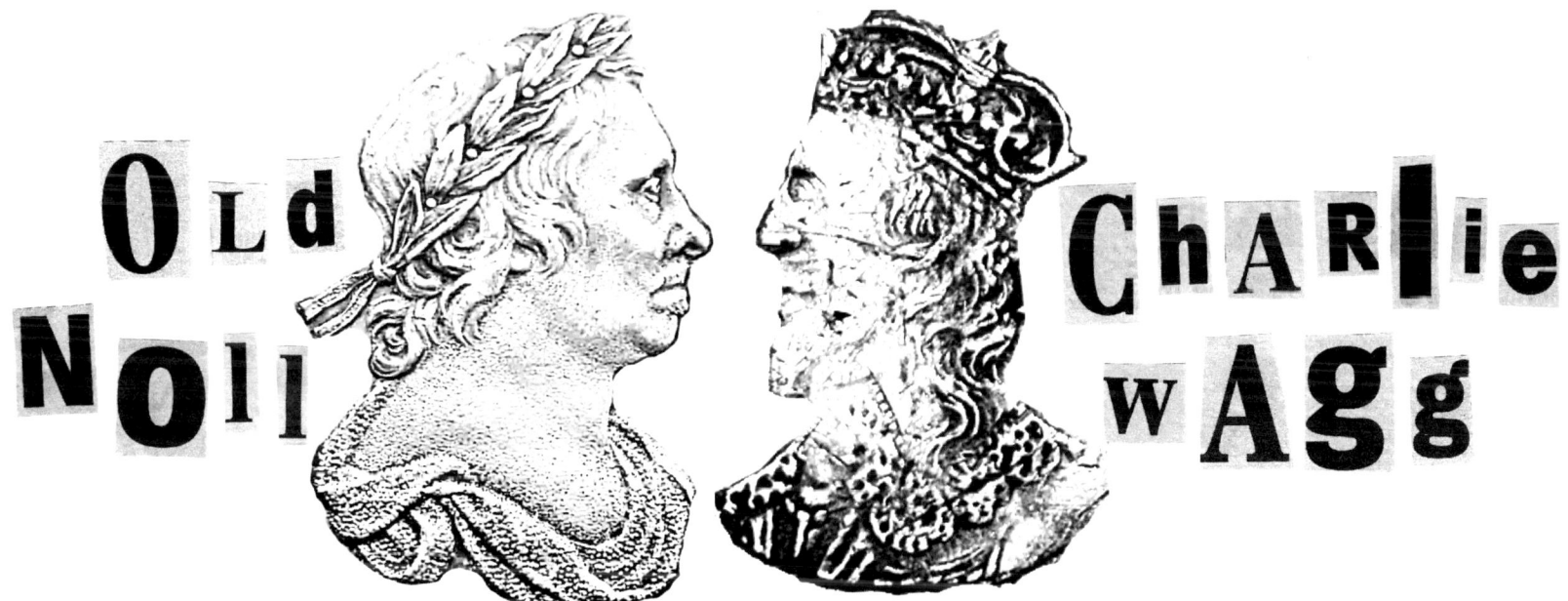

Old Noll **Charlie wAgg**

at Cromwell's House
3/9/12
Graham Caley.

To Mark Whitaker

Cromwell's Talking Head

by Gareth Calway

with illustrations by Imogen Ashwin
and a preface by Trevor Ashwin

Diggers

2012

© Gareth Calway, 2012. All Rights Reserved.

Published by Diggers
35 Cawston Road, Reepham, Norwich, NR10 4LU, UK

Design by Trevor Ashwin at World Tree

Printed by Witley Press, Hunstanton

ISBN 978-0-9573960-0-5

Front cover: Oliver Cromwell's mummified head reproduced by kind permission of Dr Sarah Tarlow

Preface

What can we do about Oliver Cromwell? At the time of writing he's been dead 354 years, but he is still alive (and not just his head!). In a way, he is alive inside us all. This is because we react to him when his name is mentioned. People like him or they don't. They have FEELINGS about him.

This isn't common with famous historical rulers. We might think that Henry VIII was an awful bloke, but most people agree about this. He was cruel, greedy and tasteless. He married all those women, executing two of them on the way. There's slightly less agreement about Richard III – did he kill those little princes or didn't he? I'm afraid most people (and most historians) think he did. Who can remember the reasonable, competent kings and queens of history?

Oliver Cromwell, in this way at least, is a bit like Mrs Thatcher. You mention her name and people say something. 'Ahhhh, the Iron Lady who made Britain respected again', or perhaps 'That stiff-necked Iron Lady – so many of our problems today are her fault'.

Under a newspaper website article about some of Cromwell's possessions, readers posted comments like 'Couldn't we do with an Oliver Cromwell now to sort out this country?', and 'Still a hero of England'. The one comment critical of Cromwell was heavily voted down.

By contrast, when I mentioned to a family member that we were working on a book on Cromwell, he replied straight away: 'He sounds like a very dodgy character – didn't he abolish Christmas?'

No-one today (probably!) would suggest another Henry VIII might be good for the country, but we feel we might get somewhere with Cromwell. To many of us, he looks **sensible**.

Just look at his enemy Charles I. Cold and arrogant, but mocked for his stammer and his Scottish accent (inherited from his dad). His government was absolutely hopeless. His foreign policy in a war-torn Europe was a joke. He tried to bully his subjects as he pleased – why should he listen to Parliament, if he was God's anointed king?

Surely it was Oliver who saw the future and was 'doing the right thing'. Whose side would you have been on at the Battle of Naseby – the great battle in the heart of England in 1645 where his Ironsides broke the Royalist army for good?

Cromwell seems to have wanted a fairer, more modern nation. He fought an awful, incompetent king. He wanted freedom for people (or most people, anyway!) to believe what they liked. He was willing to negotiate and make deals, even with people he couldn't stand – he only backed the King's execution when he decided that Charles I was so untrustworthy that he'd go on trying to start wars as long as he remained alive. He liked music (he introduced opera to England) and supported artists and musicians. He dressed humbly, and wished artists to paint him 'warts and all'.

Cromwell also killed thousands of people in his Irish campaigns – to him and his fellow English gentlemen, Irish Catholics were scarcely human. By capturing Jamaica from the Spanish, he laid the foundations for Britain's Atlantic slave trade. As a young lawyer he protected poor farmers in the Fens from having their commons drained. But once he was in charge, he was making money from drainage himself. When certain reformers suggest that all men might vote in Cromwell's more modern England, he overpowered them and had the leaders shot.

Cromwell is confusing. Some people just know they can't stand him – they think he was a miserable killjoy and king-killer. Lots of other people start out wanting to like him, but end up discovering something awful about him. They can go so far with him, but not all the way.

Cromwell's account here only gives his side of the story. It has to. It's his dead head talking. If you can see past his Round head (or between his stern Puritan lines) to other reckonings, that's your right. But don't expect Old Noll to do it for you!

Trevor Ashwin

Chapter 1. Heading Off A Burglar

GOOD EVENING, young Master. Welcome to my Grave. You're a burglar, I see. And you've been digging up a National treasure.

And now you're in a deep hole. Face to face with a hacked off Head of Security. So deep, you're never getting out again.

What's that you're screaming? 'I meant no disrespect to the Crown, Mr Head, but I got mouths to feed!'?

The Crown? Who said anything about the Crown? This treasure belongs to the *Nation*.

I've got a face like a sow's what? What do you expect? I'm *dead*.

The name's Oliver, by the way. Oliver Cromwell. Pleased to meat you. They put an axe through my neck 350 years ago. Eight swings of the butcher's blade before they got my bloodless head off. I was never so hacked off in my life!

Why did they do it? I chopped off the King's head. So his son chopped off mine.

No. I am not having a laugh. I can't. And you'll be laughing on the other side of my face if I get any more of your cheek. Me and fifty-eight soldiers chopped off the head of King Charles I. In 1649. The only time the people of England ever topped a King and became the Head of their own Nation.

Am I famous? Oh yes. I'm in all the history books. And I was on the heads side of the coins until they brought the kings back. Have I been on I'm A Celebrity? Son, I'd rather eat my own face. Can you have an autograph? Not something I can really put my hand to …

May you shake my hand instead?

If you can find it. My hand is 200 miles away, in a tomb in Yorkshire, along with what's left of my body.

How about a nose rub? There you go. Now we're talking!

Now *you're* famous. Only the special ones go head to head with me. Or pick what used to be my brains. Or find out where my headless body is.

But, over the thirty minutes, you'll hear it all. And then you'll be a celebrity. Until you die.

Oh stop yowling like a scared cat. What? You're 'too young to die'. You 'didn't mean nuffin?' You was just on the Cambridge college tour, honest guvnor, and you got lorst?'

At midnight? Six feet underground? Pull the other one, mate. If you can find it.

Not your lucky day? No, son, but it is mine. September 3. The day God and I won my great battles in 1649, 1650 and 1651. The day my soul went to heaven in 1658. The day this spike through my head was hit by a thunderbolt and started the Great Fire Of London in 1666. That'll teach Londoners to chop my head off and put it up on a roof!

My lucky day. But you make your own luck, son.

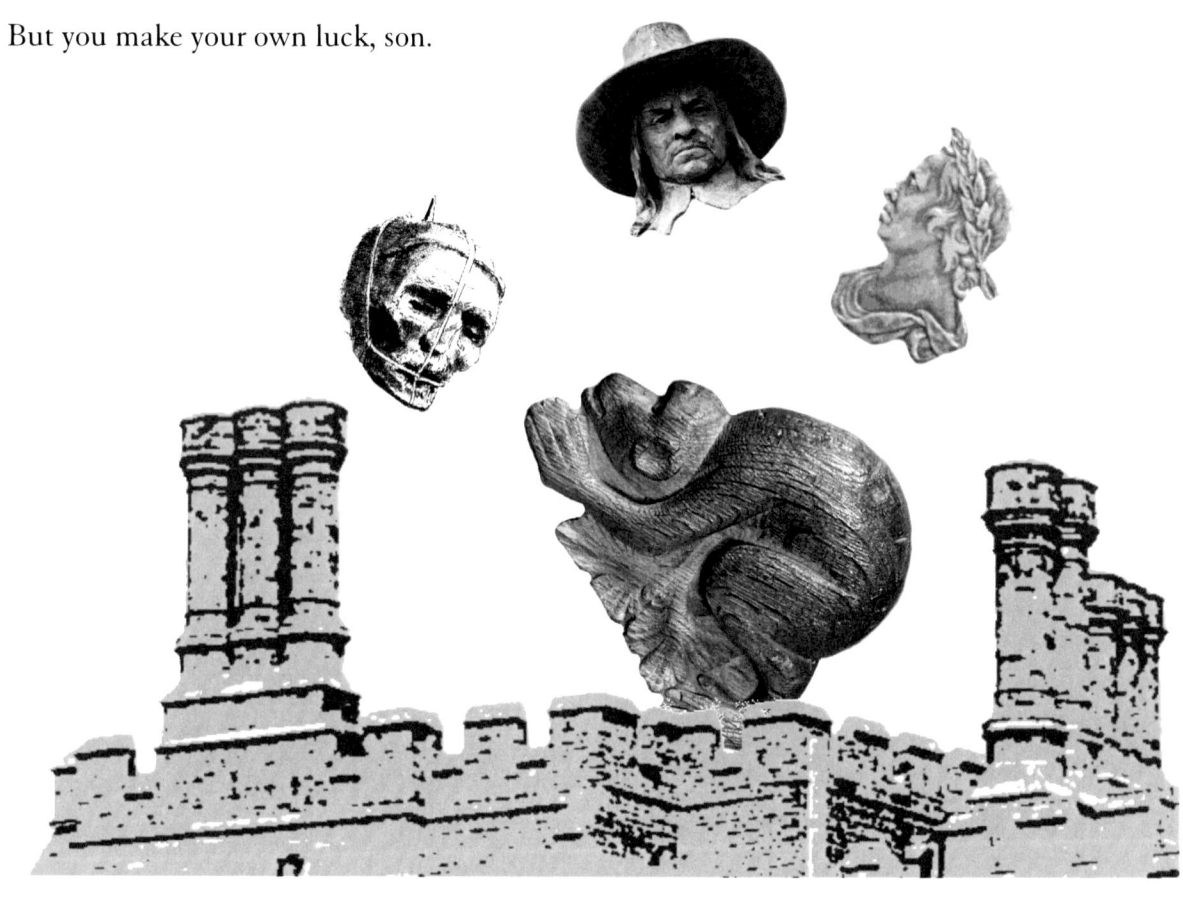

'So the baby was saved to grow up to be a great man'

Chapter 2. Heading Off On Holiday

I MADE IT MY lucky day. My annual holiday. Or, as I used to call it, holy day. And every September 3 since 1659, I've had a get together with my bones.

You can join us. No. I insist. I said NO. I INSIST. Put that national treasure down and we'll head north. To Newburgh. Yorkshire.

You don't like Newburgh? It's not the sunniest holiday home, true. And, frankly, a bit dead. Especially in Bod's bolt hole.

Pull that postcard out of my chops. It's from Bod (my body). Read it.

You can't read? You should learn to read. People can't mis-lead you so much when you can read. All right. I'll read it.

'Bod's Bolt Hole, Friday. Dear Head, Wish I was there. I'm sweating green seepage like a dead pig and nothing makes sense without you. I need to freshen up. It's like worms have been nibbling my bits for three and a half centuries. Not to mention spiders. And centipedes. And maggots.

And the rats! – gross.

And the *endless* cold and damp is wearing me down. *Really* getting on my nerves, muscles, sinews, gristle, veins, bones …'

(Bod goes on a bit but he's got a lot of time on his hands. Needs to get out more.)

'That mummy cloth they wound us in, in 1658? As much use as a wet blanket on a funny bone at Christmas. I'll catch my mouldering Death up here.

Can't wait for our stroll down Memory Lane on September 3. Bring some nibbles for yourself. And something I can get down my neck.

Give my best to Spike,

Bod x.'

Chapter 3. A Royal Bighead

WHAT ARE *YOU* shivering for, Master Burglar? I'm little more than skin and bone these days, I'm not going to eat you. Much. I can't. A crowd kicked my teeth out in 1661. Just after they chopped my head off.

Will you please shut your rude fat gob when you yowl! And put your tonsils away.

I am NOT giving you the evils! I can't. A flock of Westminster Hall crows pecked my eyes out in 1661.

Not my idea of heaven. Spiked on a twenty foot oak pole on top of a roof for 25 years. With a splitting headache.

Oh you think that's fair do you? For killing the 'poor old king'? Shall I tell you what the King did to poor fenmen like you? He stole their fields. And when *they* had to steal to feed their families, he chopped their ears off. What about a caution? That *was* the caution.

And when the poor were so hungry they stole again – the King hanged them.

Harsh, you think? Mean? Small-minded? Stupid? Cruel? Wrong?

I thought so too. But that king didn't. He thought anything a king did was right. Like he thought any stupid cruel idea in his head was clever. 'We have a crown of jewels and velvet on *Our* head.' he said, 'therefore, We are God's gift.'

A right royal big head, yes.

Until we chopped it off.

CROWN CROWS

'The World Turn'd Upside Down'

Chapter 4. Roundheads You Lose

WE DRAGGED THE KING from his fine palace of Windsor.

We did not call him King. We called him Charles Stuart. Murderer. Traitor. Burner. Spoiler. Mischief-maker. Nation-destroyer.

Liar. Sneak.

He made war on his own country for seven years. Our people's army was called the Roundheads. It was led by Sir Thomas Fairfax and me.

The King's army was called the Cavaliers.

The Roundheads won.

We made peace. The King broke the peace deal. So we beat him again, in a second war. Everyone knew he was a liar now.

'Stand down as King and let your son take your place.'

'Never.'

'Then you must stand trial as a traitor.'

'I am your lawful K-k-king. (He always stammered when crossed.) You c-c-cannot try me. If you do, you bring the J-judgement of G-god on this land.'

He spent weeks combing his long curls and bleating about his 'c-c-c-crucifix-ion.'

We told him, 'You are not God's Chosen. You are a tyrant with the blood of England on your hands. We sentence you to death.'

He stood there. Not a King now. Just a short man in a black hat and grey beard. His face looked thin and ill.

'Let him speak!' said John Downes. Downes was one of only fifty nine men who signed the King's death warrant.

(Fairfax would not sign it.)

'What's wrong with you?' I answered, 'He is a traitor and a tyrant!'

Charles Stuart chuckled nervously. 'So I am not allowed to sp-speak!'

I said. 'You can speak on the scaffold!'

With Borage and with Bloodstone

we fought Day and Night

Chapter 5. The King's Speech.

WE BUILT A SCAFFOLD in Whitehall. We had nothing to hide. We invited a crowd.

January 30 1649. A cold morning. Charles was trembling. 'With c-cold, not f-fear,' he said. He asked for a second shirt.

He dressed himself neatly in his two shirts, not a hair out of place. He stared at the block. He stopped stammering. 'The block to the wooden platform is extremely low. May it be raised a little?'

'No.' said a soldier.

'Why not?'

'No reason.'

He had a paper in his hand. 'I have not been allowed to make a speech. May I make it now?' His head turned on its swan neck. To me. Death.

'Yes.'

He made his speech. A history lesson. 'I am the King and you are my Subjects. A subject and his King are clean different things-'

'Cut off his head with the crown upon it!'

He lay down over the low block. A few grey hairs strayed out from his white cap. He tucked them back up neatly.

I raised my head to the axeman. 'Do it boldly, Brandon!'

'Oliver, no!' begged Fairfax.

The blade came down.

The head shot off into the bloody basket. Brandon held it aloft by its hair. We felt blood spray their eyes and lips. We tasted royal blood. The army cheered.

The crowd didn't. They groaned.

Soft-headed fools.

Which one will YOU choose?

I said. 'Men will remember this axe blow forever. Good men with pride. Only tyrants with fear.'

I was patient all my life with good men. Men who tried hard to be good.

I only killed bad men. Traitors. Liars. Thieves. Kings.

Why are you shivering, Burglar?

Chapter 6. Head Honcho

I RAN THE COUNTRY for ten years. They asked me to be King. I said 'We no longer need Kings.'

We didn't. Until I died.

'Bury him as a King!' they said.

'Over my dead body!' I said. They did it anyway.

Two years later, they invited Charles I's son back to be King Charles II. I turned in my grave.

Charles II heard me. He sent his men to dig me up.

'Do you mind? I said. Some of us are trying to rest in peace!'

They took me on a coffin ride to the *King's Head* in Holborn.

Bradshaw and my son-in-law Major General Ireton were at the bar. Bradshaw was the sober Judge who sentenced the Charles I to death. The old rotter looked as stiff as ever. He'd been dead two years. Ireton died of a fever fighting the Irish in 1651. His ten year corpse stood to attention. He looked well-preserved for his age.

'Long live King Charles II!' shouted the King's men from the straw. They were dead drunk. We were dead unimpressed.

'What's the matter, Cromwell?' hiccupped a drunk, on his back in the straw. 'Too stuck up to drink our new King's health?'

I was never against drinking. 'To keep wine out of the country lest men be drunk?' Ha! When they turned my old house in Ely into the *Cromwell Arms*, it wasn't the first drink it had ever seen! I even did a bit of brewing once. And my redcoats and I never went into a battle without a pint or two inside us. We never lost a charge either.

Everyone drank beer in those days. Morning, noon and night. The whole country was merry the whole time.

We drank beer and wine because the London water killed you. But I never drank to a King. And I never drank like a pig at trough.

These Royalists did. The bar queue was longer than the King's drinking bill. A man came in, waiting to be served. He pointed at me. 'Is that Cromwell?'

The drunk on the floor broke wind and belched, "Good morning, Sham! Yesh!"

'Sam. Mr Pepys to you. How long has my Lord Cromwell been there?' he asked.

'Four daysh, Peeps!' hooted a drunk from the floor. 'And he *still* hasn't been sherved!'

The Royalists laughed themselves sick

'I can't wait that long for a drink,' said Sam. 'And I will be reporting your behaviour in my diary.'

Bradshaw wasn't looking well. Green. Mouldy. Sweating blood and pus. And his backside – faugh!

I dripped into his ear. 'You weren't preserved like me and Ireton were you?'

'How do you know?' he dribbled.

'You smell.'

'I do not smell,' he grinned. 'I stink!'

'Someone's pinched my nose!' shouted Ireton.

'Then how do you smell?' I asked.

'Not as bad as Bradshaw!'

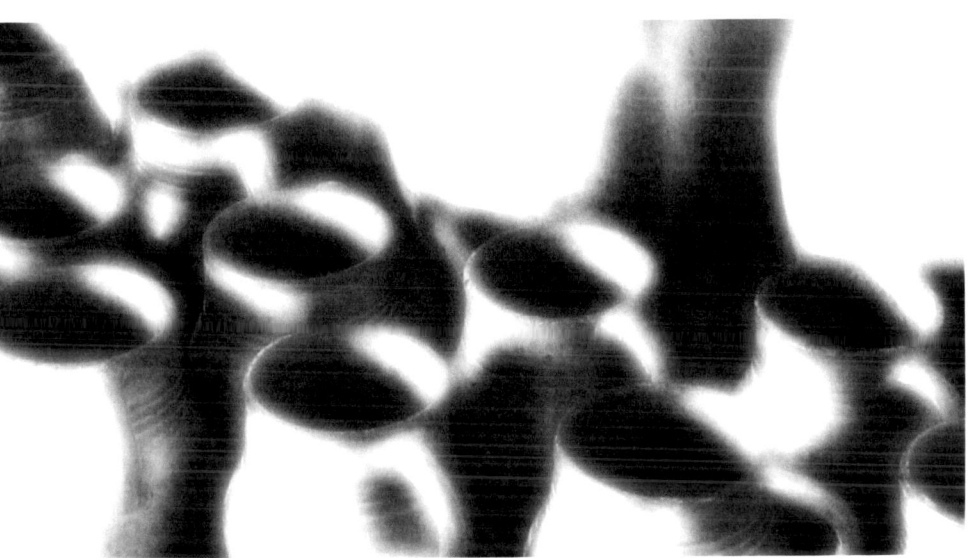

Chapter 7. Off Our Heads

IRETON, BRADSHAW AND I were leaking towards the fireplace. The drunks took a leak on the floor.

'Use the fireplace, you pigs!' said the barman.

'You kick Cromwell's crutch,' said a Royalist. 'I'll punch Bradshaw's face in.' He threw a punch and his fist stuck. He plucked it free.

Bradshaw's eye came away in his ale. Followed by his guts. And some of Bradshaw's.

I leaned over and winked at the Royalist. 'Bradshaw wasn't preserved. You're punching a rotten cheese.' My mouth oozed forward over his nose and mouth.

He tore his face from mine with a faint suck.

They brought sledges outside *The King's Head* and dragged us in our coffins to Tyburn. Things looked grave. We were jeered and stoned and yelled and pelted and barked and spat at. And, in the case of anyone close enough to get a whiff of Bradshaw, sicked on.

'Nice to get out of that booze-hole and into the fresh air,' said Bradshaw. 'That barman had the worst BO in London!'

We arrived at Tyburn Tree at 9 am. Heroes of the Republic. They hanged us like criminals.

Me, fresh as a daisy.

Ireton, ten years buried, hanging like a dried rat. Except for the stuff streaming out of his backside.

Bradshaw with his nose and the fingers of his right hand rotted off. In a pus-soaked winding sheet.

For six hours the crowd laughed its head off. Then they hacked off ours.

Bradshaw's kind of fell off. Ireton's snapped off like a dried apple. Mine took eight cuts.

chop headache seepage spray brainless aloft

pelted cheered snapped green hacked guts

'More cloth round his neck than a bishop. Stiff-necked pig!'

'DON'T call me a bishop!'

They smashed the end of my nose off. They knocked out most of my teeth.

'Hey, watch the face! I'm supposed to be getting it in the neck!'

Some jokers cut off Bradshaw's toes and threw them to the crowd. One pocketed my ear. Finally they got through my collarbone. My head hit the basket. They held it up to the cheering crowds.

They kicked our headless bodies into a deep pit under the gallows. One body got lost in the crowd.

The King's man looked worried. 'As long as we ditched Cromwell?'

'The bod in the posh green cloth? Yes. We did.'

Chapter 8. Heads Up!

'HEADS UP LADS!' I said. 'Here come the metal spikes!'

'Wh-what are they going to do with those?' Bradshaw was falling apart.

'Pull yourself together, man. It can't hurt you.'

'I can't think of a worse place to get a spike!' said Bradshaw's head.

'I can,' said Ireton's. 'But luckily it's down there in the pit.'

Bradshaw closed his sockets. They spiked and hoisted him. He didn't notice.

'Hey up, Bradshaw! You're on!'

'On what?'

'A twenty foot oak pole on the top of Westminster Hall.'

Bradshaw went green.

Then it was my turn. You could see half of London up on that roof. Until the birds got your eyes. I always said the same crowd who cheered my speeches would cheer as loud for my hanging. Now they did.

Up came Ireton to make 'three bold traitors.' Me on one side of Bradshaw. Ireton on the other.

"Not so bad once you're up!' bled Ireton. 'Is Bradshaw's head in the middle because he was head of the court that chopped off the King's head?'

My tongue was spiked.

'Just nod.'

I nodded.

We made headlines in all the papers.

'King-Killing Killjoys Cut Down To Size By Common Crowd.' (The Royalist Times)

'Woundheads Warned By Wicked Woyals' (The Puritan)

'Up Yours Crom!' (The Sun).

'Bouncy Actress Busts King's Bed.' (The Stage)

(Well maybe not The Stage.)

None of them got the story right. You will, Master Burglar. You will trace the cut through Bod's collarbone to this dirty great chop in my neck. The last of eight. Put your finger on it. Of course you can. It's only like touching a frog.

That's right. It wasn't my body in the pit. My family did a switch while the crowd's back was turned. It was Bradshaw's. One whiff should have told them. His body was the rotting green of a two year corpse. Mine was the sweet green of royal grave-cloth.

And it was already heading north in the back of a cart. If a headless body can head north.

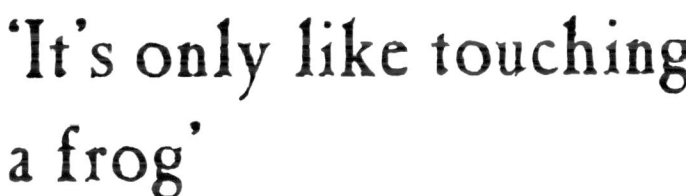

'It's only like touching a frog'

Chapter 9. Headless

'CAN A BODY ask where you're taking it?'

'Yorkshire.'

'HA! THEY WANT SOME MORE DO THEY?'

'Bod! Wind your neck in! There's a price on your head.'

'My head's in London. On a spike.'

'Your body then. And *our* heads. Think about it.'

'Think? What with? OI! YORKSHIRE. MY NEW MODEL ARMY SMASHED YOURS AT MARSTON MOOR AND I'LL DO IT AGAIN!'

'We risk our heads for his body and he yells his neck off!'

'I never thought a relative of mine would be so spineless! Where's your strong Cromwell jaw?'

'Where's yours? What happened to that fully Roundheaded Oliver we loved? That wise head on strong shoulders? Always thinking of others.'

'They spiked it. I'm brainless brawn now. I *can't* think.'

'So? It's a gut feeling, a no-brainer. You're a rebel hero, the model of a King-killer. The Royalists want your relics trampled out of sight, out of mind.'

'Then why did they dig me up? COME ON YORKSHIRE IF YOU THINK YOU'RE HARD ENOUGH!'

'Shhh! Because you were buried as a King. In King Henry VII's tomb. *They* want your head on a traitor's spike instead. And your remains in a common pit. Spat on and walked over. An example to anyone who even *thinks* about going head to head with a King.'

'Let them find me. I won't spill my guts to any Royalist patrol.'

'You haven't got any guts, Bod. They were scraped out with a trowel and the hole

filled with spices. Like a King. Remember?'

'LIKE A KING! ME? I HATED KINGS!'

'Shh! Stop jawing back there. Royal patrol!'

'What's all this then?'

'A dead body, Constable. What did you think it was? Oliver Cromwell?'

'Cocky southerners, eh? And what's a dead body doing in the back of your cart?'

'Nothing much. It's Uncle Bod. We're taking him home for a decent family burial.'

'Where's his head?'

'It got held up in London …'

Chapter 10. Chop Chop

SO, MASTER BURGLAR, now you know where me and Bod live. Which means I have to chop your head off.

What's that? Your children need their father? You love your wife? You'll get an honest job?

Oh shut your noise and listen. All right. My worst enemy would tell you I always gave people a choice. And a second chance. Even the King. Make sure you take yours.

It's this. Next time you come to my old college, make sure you can read the signs. And if I catch you with your hands in the treasure again, it's the bolt hole in Yorkshire for you, with brainless Bod.

How long for? In Death-initely.

No you can't have a lift! I'm heading back to heaven. And you're climbing back out of this hole on your own hands and feet with your head held high.

Well don't just stand there! I'm giving you a head start. Leg it.

Chop chop. Before I change my mind.

Cheeky Burglar!

Notes On The Illustrations

Front cover: The mummified head of Oliver Cromwell. After his death on 3 September 1658, his body was buried at Westminster Abbey. At the Restoration of Charles II, however, it was exhumed. On 30 January 1661 the body (along with those of two other men who had signed Charles I's death warrant) was 'executed' at Tyburn. After being hanged, it was beheaded and the head displayed on a spike at Westminster Hall. The top of the spike is still visible in this picture. After a mysterious history it eventually fell into the hands of a Canon Wilkinson. An examination in 1934 proved beyond reasonable doubt that the head is Cromwell's. On Wilkinson's death in 1960 it was buried in a secret location at Sidney Sussex College, Cambridge.

We are grateful to Dr Sarah Tarlow for allowing us to use this image, taken from the definitive report on the head published by Pearson and Morant in 1934. Karl Pearson and Geoffrey Morant, 'The Wilkinson Head of Oliver Cromwell and Its Relationship to Busts, Masks and Painted Portraits', *Biometrika* 29 (3).

Frontispiece: Old Noll and Charlie Wagg are Fenland nicknames for Oliver Cromwell and King Charles I. These nose-to-nose characters were originally solitary figures on the 'heads' side of coins.

Page 2: 'When Oliver was still a baby, he had been taken to see his grandfather [and] a monkey came lolloping into the room and right up to the cradle. The monkey thought that the baby would be a lovely plaything, so he seized him and ran away with him. Leaping, swinging, clinging with hand and tail, he swung himself and his prize up to the flat lead roof of the house. Soon the baby was missed, and when it was discovered that the monkey was playing with him on the roof, the whole household was thrown into a state of confusion. Beds and blankets were brought out and placed on the ground ... in case the monkey should drop or throw him down. But the monkey was careful, and presently he brought Oliver safely to the ground again. So the baby was saved to grow up to be a great man.' H. E. Marshall (1876–1941), *Through Great Britain and Ireland with Cromwell*. The roof shown here is that of Hinchingbrooke House, Huntingdon, where the legendary incident took place.

Page 5: 'A flock of Westminster Hall crows pecked my eyes out in 1661.' The 'crows' here are much-loved earrings – a nod to the Cavalier spirit!

Page 7: A Fen tradition held that Cromwell's soldiers were able to fight day and night without rest as long as they had borage leaves to chew. It was also firmly believed in the Fens that every one of Cromwell's soldiers carried a bloodstone and that it was due to this that so simple a life-saver came into Fenland. These stones were multicoloured glass marbles threaded onto a yard of silk cord, tied with three knots at three inch intervals. Whenever a deep gash had to be treated quickly the bloodstone was fastened tightly round the limb to arrest the bleeding. The 'bloodstone' here is a marble unearthed in a Norfolk garden, while the cord has been plaited from yarn dyed with woad, associated with the warriordom and bravery of East Anglia's Eceni tribe.

Page 9: The *Cromwell* ice lolly is modelled on the statue that stands outside the Palace of Westminster in London, while the statue that provided the template for the *King Charles* resides in a niche on the exterior of a house in Little Walsingham, Norfolk.

Page 13: The notorious 'Tyburn Tree' was once thought to have stood next to Marble Arch in west London. Recent research suggests that it probably lay a little to the north-west, in what is now leafy Connaught Square.

Page 15: As a young man, Cromwell paid several visits to Heydon Hall near Reepham in Norfolk. It is said that Oliver enjoyed climbing a particular oak tree in the park, which although weatherbeaten still stands and is known as Cromwell's Oak. The 'spike' is a twig from this tree. On top of the spike is the mummified 'frog' companion of an early twentieth century wisewoman.

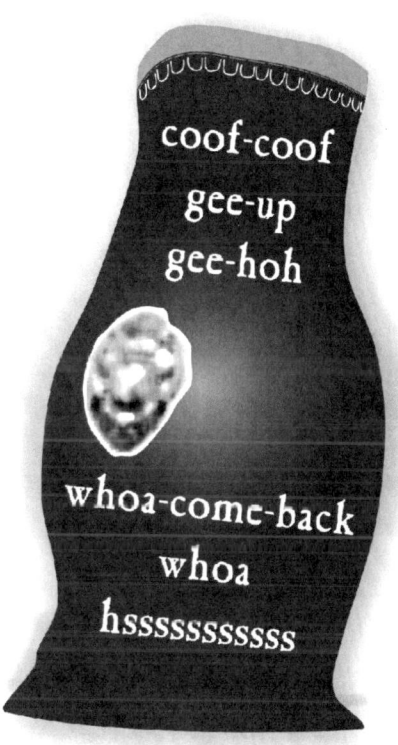

Page 17: Blome's map of Yorkshire (printed in 1672) shows Newburgh. Does Cromwell's headless body really lie in a vault at the priory? Is there *really* a party there every 3 September?

Page 18: Cromwell's head surveys the scene from the top of an oak tree in Heydon Park, Norfolk. It is said that he enjoyed climbing this tree as a young man. The other oak tree, hiding the future Charles II in its heart, is from a Royal Oak pub sign. The Royal Oak is thought to be the most popular name for an English pub.

Page 21: When his favourite horse, Blackjack, died, Cromwell had the skin made up into several leather jugs. One of these re-emerged as recently as September 2011. The words here are from Huntingdonshire horse-lore and address the horse at each stage of a ride from saddling-up to the grooming session afterwards.

Page 22: The final appearance of the Cromwell Oak at Heydon – with its 'indwelling spirit'!

Back cover: It was an old Fen custom to show a man how unpopular he was after he had broken the Fen code of never letting down or betraying his fellow fenmen, by drawing on his door a certain sign. Cromwell's house in Ely is daubed with this sign, representing a stem of hemp and a willow stake; 'a reminder of the days when, if a man hung himself, he was buried at the cross-roads with a stake through his body. Hemp was used for making … the hangman's rope … a gentle hint that the man should go and hang himself.' Enid Porter; *Cambridgeshire Customs and Folklore*.

21